Local Wildlife Series : 4

(Series Editor : Tony Soper)

WILDLIFE
OF THE
SALCOMBE AND
KINGSBRIDGE
ESTUARY

In the same series as this volume:

Wildlife of the Dart Estuary : Tony Soper
Wildlife of the Exe Estuary : Stan Davies
Wildlife of the Fal Estuary : Roger Burrows

Front Cover: General view of the Estuary
(*Photo by Bryan Ashby*)

Cirl Bunting, reproduced from an engraving by Elizabeth Dorville,
which appeared as the frontispiece of George Montagu's
Ornithological Dictionary, published London, 1802.

WILDLIFE OF THE SALCOMBE AND KINGSBRIDGE ESTUARY

Gordon Waterhouse

Photographs by Bryan Ashby
Line drawings by Mick Loates
Maps by Hilary Soper

Series Editor: Tony Soper

Harbour Books : Dartmouth

1992

First published in Great Britain in 1992 by Harbour Books, 12 Fairfax Place, Dartmouth, Devon TQ6 9AE

British Library Cataloguing in Publication Data

A catalogue record for this book is available from the British Library

---

Photoset in 10/11pt Times
Printed in Great Britain by BPCC Wheatons Ltd, Exeter

CONTENTS

My thanks
to Hilary and Tony Soper, who encouraged me to write
Wildlife of the Salcombe and Kingsbridge Estuary,
to Bruce Coward our publisher,
to Bryan and Jane Ashby for their photographs,
to Mick Loates for his evocative illustrations and
to Barbara, my long-suffering wife.

This book is dedicated to them and to the many other naturalists with whom I have walked and sailed the estuary; also to those, like George Montagu, who walked its shores before us.

FOREWORD

The Salcombe-Kingsbridge estuary is not an estuary at all. Technically it is an inlet, a ria, a drowned valley formed by rises in sea level since the last ice age. But for the practical purposes of a field naturalist it makes sense to regard it as an estuary. Perhaps there was once a Kingsbridge river seduced into joining the present-day Avon and diverted to the sea at Bantham, perhaps it is simply the result of the sea exploiting a weakness in the coastal schist. Whatever the cause, the result is an estuary with very little fresh water flowing into it, and this has a profound effect on the fauna and flora: it is an unusually marine-dominated one. It is a muddy estuary, though the seaward end boasts golden sandy beaches. At high water the mud is completely covered to blossom into a huge 'lake'.

Visitors, and even a few locals to their shame, sometimes wish that the 'plug' could be left in and the high water lake become permanent. But, quite apart from the ecological changes which would turn the watery expanse into a reed swamp, this is to misunderstand the whole beauty of the estuary system, with the ebb and flow of the tide painting an ever-changing scene and varying the pattern of enjoyment. In the summer, sailors enjoy the challenge of working the tidal currents and avoiding the ignominy of a few hours stuck on the mud. In the winter, great numbers of wildfowl and shorebirds invade from their northern breeding grounds. When the tide is out they work the mud for worms and shells and shrimps. When the tide is in, they find a sheltered roost while the flounders and mullet take their turn to feed. On a good tide, a grey seal may come up for a fish or two; even an osprey may join us for a while.

Gordon Waterhouse knows the wildlife of this patch better than anyone and this book is the fruit of many years of diligent research, to say nothing of several pairs of worn-out boots! Follow in his wake and you will be richly rewarded. But, as always, give a thought to the well-being of our fellow-creatures and take great care not to disturb them unduly.

December 1991   Tony Soper

GEORGE MONTAGU (1753–1815)
A memoir

'The days of darkness are now past, when the researches of the naturalist were considered as trivial and uninteresting.'
GEORGE MONTAGU *Testacea Britannica* 1803

George Montagu, one of the fathers of natural history in Britain, spent the last 16 years of his life in Kingsbridge. During this period he published his major works, *An ornithological dictionary* and *Testacea Britannica* (a survey of seashore and estuary life). In 1789 he had written to Gilbert White, 'Was I not bound by conjugal attachment, I should like to ride my hobby to distant parts.' The distant parts he later chose were the South Hams of Devon. He came, with Eliza Dorville his 'friend of science', as he called his mistress, to rent Knowle Cottage, at the top of Fore Street, in 1798.

In 1800 he discovered the cirl bunting, never before identified in Britain, nesting around **Kingsbridge**. Two years later he discovered a new bird of prey, breeding on the gorse-covered slopes near his home. He named it the ashy-coloured falcon. After his death it was renamed Montagu's harrier. These, and many other birds, he reared in aviaries in his garden, to study their changes of plumage and behaviour.

Eliza obviously enjoyed the menagerie. Choughs then occurred in Devon and George Montagu kept one for several years. It was very attached to Eliza and would sit on the back of her chair for hours. One can imagine the scene at Knowle Cottage garden, when the gardener had out his box of nails and the chough would come up behind him and carry off a beakful. Children must have been in the habit of coming along to see the birds, for Montagu refers to the chough's aversion to them and how it would try to drive them away.

In June 1815, Montagu trod on a rusty nail left by men doing repairs to his house. He contracted lock-jaw and died, in much pain, the day after the battle of Waterloo.

The remains of his collection of stuffed birds is still stored by the British Museum. Most of his collection of shells is at Exeter Museum.

Portrait of George Montagu by kind permission of the Linnean Society

He is responsible for describing more than 50 species new to science and his name is remembered in the scientific name of more than a dozen birds, crustaceans, snails or fish. George Montagu was truly the founder of the scientific study of wildlife in the **Salcombe and Kingsbridge Estuary** and we are, perhaps literally, treading in his footsteps.

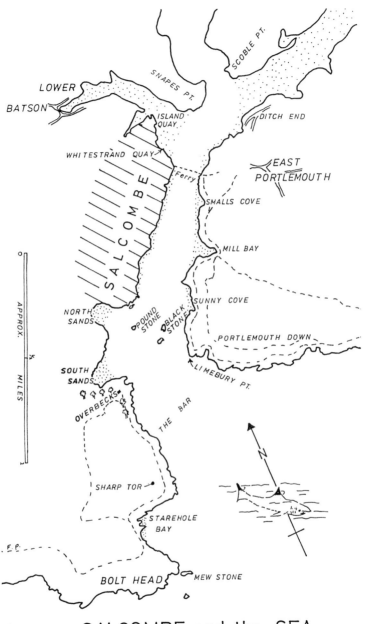

SALCOMBE and the SEA

I

FROM THE SEA TO SALCOMBE

From **Bolt Tail** to **Start Point** are 10 miles of beautiful coast, sculpted from rocks of hard schist, sparkling grey, jagged mica schist and pale green curves and honeycombs of horneblende schist.

Between **Bolt Head** and **Limebury Point** is the narrow entrance to **Salcombe Harbour**. The waters below are rich in plankton, sand-eels, mackerel, pollack and young bass. Near the sea bed rays, especially thornbacks, feed on the smaller fish; blennies, gobies, rocklings, butterfish and wrasse. Montagu was the first to sort out the differences between the sexes and species of rays. In crannies and holes round the **Black Stone** conger eels are especially plentiful.

Birds come to feed on the plankton and fish. The snake-necked birds sitting in the water and diving repeatedly are mostly shags. The shag is smaller than the cormorant. In breeding plumage it is all black, has a yellow gape visible at the base of the bill and a curly black crest. The young birds are brown, with a creamy throat and neck. They are principally fishers of the open coast, specializing in mid-water fish like pollack and mackerel. There are always about half a dozen over **The Bar** and in autumn there may be up to 100. Their dives average 40 seconds but they can be under water for up to three minutes.

The Bar is built of sand and stretches across the estuary from near **Limebury Point**. As the water becomes shallower, waves pile up dangerously, if the wind is southerly and against the ebb. In such conditions it is a hazardous place for boats. White horses rear up and their crests are blown into smoking manes. The Salcombe lifeboat was capsized here in 1916 and 13 of her crew of 15 were drowned. It was here that Tennyson may have felt the inspiration to write his poem 'Crossing The Bar'.

Cormorants concentrate their fishing in the harbour and estuary but also use the open coast. They specialize in bottom feeding fish such as flounders and eels. The cormorants are big, black and thick-necked; in breeding plumage they sport a white throat patch and a white thigh patch. The head, particularly in older males, may be suffused with silvery white. The first year birds are brown with often quite startlingly white bellies, which make them look like their relative the brown pelican.

Below Bar Lodge, cormorants use some of the trees clinging to the cliff face as a roost. On the rocks off **Sunny Cove** and **North** and **South Sands** both shags and cormorants can be seen, with wings outstretched to dry.

Sandwich terns fish for sand-eels here. They are beautiful, white birds, nick-named sea-swallows for their elegant flight and forked tails, an image spoiled by a call like a creaking gate. They poise in mid-air and drop head first into the sea to catch their fish. Their chief breeding territories are the sand dunes of north and east Britain. Some pass through the estuary in spring but they are most common from July to September, when up to 75 have been seen together perched on the rocks off **Portlemouth Down**. In the winter they migrate to the rich waters off the coasts of Angola and South Africa.

Between **Bolt Head** and **The Bar** the commonest gull is the herring gull, with a few great black-backs and, in summer, lesser black-backs. From early spring and throughout the summer there are some kittiwakes. Their dancing flight makes them look like white butterflies but with completely black wing tips. Their black feet sometimes trail the water as they flutter before feeding. The nearest established nesting colony is at **Start Point** but in some years there is a small colony near **Starehole Bay** and then you may hear the 'kittiwa-a-a-ke' cry that gives the gull its name. All winter they ride out the storms in mid-Atlantic.

Occasional gannets come fishing close to shore, gliding on their white, black-tipped wings and plummeting into the sea with a spurt of foam. A few black and white auks, guillemots and razorbills, also fish here.

Overbecks museum and gardens, belonging to the National Trust, makes an excellent starting point from which to explore the cliff paths. Overbecks has a short but fascinating history. Half the building is now a museum, with unexpected and ethereal background music, and the other half a youth hostel. The dining room of the hostel doubles as a tearoom in the summer and makes a welcome resting place at the end of a day's walking. In the garden, amidst a beautiful herbaceous border, is a delightful bronze statue of a girl holding a bird's nest. From the garden are fine views up the estuary. Booklets on the garden and cliff walks are for sale in the museum.

Down the road from **Overbecks** a track leads seaward, through woodland, out onto the cliff path where the oaks are gnarled and stunted by wind pruning, like those of Wistman's Wood on Dartmoor. Growing by the path is a south-western speciality, climbing corydalis; a sprawling plant like fumitory but with creamy flowers. This was

Coastal flowers below Sharp Tor

a plant recorded by Sarah Prideaux Fox in her book 'Kingsbridge Estuary', published in 1864. Along this path to **Bolt Head** she also mentioned ' . . . a great variety of such plants as will thrive with but little soil to support them — foxgloves, bell heather, sheepsbit scabious, broom, burnet rose, stinking iris, butchers' broom, dodder, bloody cranesbill, English stonecrop and spring and autumn squills.' All of these can still be found.

Where a jagged ridge of schist seems to bar the way, pause to enjoy the view. A steep, grassy slope falls away to the sea. In March and April it is sprinkled, like salt, with the flowers of early scurvy grass. Blue violets and scattered spring squills edge the path. In May and June it is pink with thrift and vivid with scattered patches of yellow kidney vetch, white sea campion and ox-eye daisy. Later in the summer the slope is dappled by the white umbels of wild carrot and bright yellow splashes of birdsfoot trefoil. On the trefoil leaves may be seen the small, green and hairy caterpillars of the common blue butterfly or the larger black and yellowish-green, chequered caterpillars of the six-spot burnet moth. Hugging the turf are mounds of sharp-scented, pink-flowered thyme. Below is a lumpy stack of rock, capped with orange lichen and surrounded by foam. The scene could be on a bird island, like Skokholm, and you half expect a party of puffins to land on the thrift-dappled slope and disappear down rabbit burrows. Sadly, no puffins breed on mainland Devon these days.

13

Steps and a narrow path were blasted out of the schist spur by Lord Courtenay in the last century. Ragged pinnacles tower above. By the rocks are the reddish, succulent leaves and pink, starry blossom of English stonecrop. And on the rocks themselves are many lichens, including the bright, lime-green patches of *Rhizocarpon geographicum*.

Having rounded the corner, where the edge of the path is protected by railings, a different community of plants is on display. Portland spurge and bell heather become common, and also that fine wild geranium, the bloody cranesbill. There are occasional plants of saw-wort and carline thistle. Below the railings look out for butchers' broom, a plant with stiff branches which were used for sweeping out the butchers' scraps. From the ivy which grows here spring up brownish-purple spikes of ivy broomrape; a parasitic plant feeding from the host.

An extensive area of dwarf privet attracts many butterflies. There may be peacocks, red admirals, small tortoiseshells, dark-green fritillaries, painted ladies, common blues, small coppers, marbled whites, gatekeepers and walls. And just as Sarah Prideaux Fox described, more than a century ago, the meadow brown, small heath, large and small skippers, small pearl-bordered fritillary, ringlet, green hairstreak, grayling and clouded yellow can still be found. Silver-studded blues are here in small numbers but the large blue, which she said was here 'and in very few places in England', is here no more.

Following the path round towards **Bolt Head**, the steep slopes are clothed with bracken. Before the bracken grows tall, bluebells, all too briefly, turn the slopes blue. It is immaterial to the bluebells whether it is an oak-wood or bracken that provides the shade they require after the flowering period. Pignut is a feathery-leaved little umbellifer that needs similar conditions. It is the food-plant of the chimney sweeper moth. This small moth is day-flying, like the six-spot burnet and coloured sooty black.

From the promontory there are wonderful views; eastwards to the white coastguard hut on **Prawle Point** and to **Rame Head** and beyond in the west. Closer at hand the common oak eggar and drinker moth caterpillars are often seen feeding near the path, and this area is a site for the rare grass eggar. The caterpillar has longer, more golden hairs than the oak eggar but with similar black bands on the body. Another speciality is the fly-like thrift clearwing moth, whose larvae cause brown patches in the crowns of thrift plants.

On the slopes above and below the path are compact cushions of summer gorse, *Ulex gallii*. A parastic plant called dodder often spreads its web of thread-like stems over the gorse bushes. It grows equally well on common gorse *Ulex europaeus*, which is especially abundant on **Portlemouth Down** and up **Starehole** valley. It is said, 'When kissing's out of season, Then gorse is out of bloom' although gorse is at its best in April. On the gorse look out for a stonechat, twitching its tail, a flock of twittering linnets or a whitethroat fluttering upwards to give its rasping summer flight song.

Below the upper path back to **Overbecks**, ravens 'cronk' as they fly, their huge beaks and wedge-shaped tails distinguishing them from the more common carrion crows. A pair nest each February on the inaccessible cliffs near **Sharp Tor**. Buzzard and kestrel still haunt the cliffs and valley near **Starehole** and, after an absence of 20 years, the peregrine has dramatically returned to this coast. You see the powerful, pigeon-like bird of prey with black moustaches curving down the cream neck, flying purposefully or swooping out of the sky at a hapless feral pigeon.

A bird of prey no longer seen is the sea eagle. In the 18th century it may have nested here. Where did Montagu obtain the two he kept in an aviary? In 1909 one was shot near **Salcombe**. As you stand near the plinth on the top of **Sharp Tor**, looking down at the wrinkled sea, it is easy to imagine Tennyson's 'Eagle' as a white-tailed sea eagle perched on the jagged crags.

Peregrine Falcon, Sharp Tor

15

To reach the eastern side of the estuary you can cross from **Salcombe** to **East Portlemouth** by ferry. From the National Trust car park at **Millbay** a path leads through attractive woodland and onto the cliff path to **Limebury Point** and beyond. The variety of flowers is similar to those on the western side. Wild madder, like a big, shiny, dark-green goosegrass, is particularly common above **Sunny Cove**. It is a food-plant of the bloody-nosed beetle. You see the wrinkled black larvae and the glossy, round beetles, which if molested 'bleed' from the mouth as a protective reflex. The cliff top at **Sunny Cove** is also one of the most prolific sites for bloody cranesbill.

There are few places that cater so satisfactorily for all ages and many interests as a sandy beach with rock pools at low tide. **Sunny Cove** is a delightful beach and **Millbay**, **Smalls Cove** and **North** and **South Sands** all have their attractions.

At the top of **Sunny Cove** beach the succulent, yellow-green sea sandwort is common and, above it, sea radish, a cousin of our garden radish. There is a patch of hoary cress; a species with grey-green leaves clasping the stem and, in April, an umbel of white flowers. It is uncommon in Devon. It is thought to have been introduced by British soldiers who emptied out their mattresses on Kentish soil after returning from the Netherlands during the Napoleonic wars.

At **Millbay** there is a small area of sand dunes stabilized by sea couch grass and a little marram grass. There are patches of sea sandwort and trailing stems of sea bindweed with its kidney-shaped leaves and pink and white trumpet flowers. In the sandy cliffs, at the edge of the dunes, sand wasps stock their burrows with paralysed flies for their grubs to feed on.

Along high water mark, sheltering under the flotsam and jetsam, are 'sandhoppers', sometimes called side-shrimps, because they lie on their sides. The species called *Talitrus saltator* was first described by Montagu. The creamy tests of sea potatoes are often washed up. These sea urchins are very common in the sand below low water mark. Jellyfish too may be stranded, sometimes in large numbers. The common jellyfish is transparent, with four bluish crescents, and measures about six inches across. The compass jellyfish, or sea nettle, is a foot or more in diameter, with 16 rich brown chevrons like the points of the compass and four long, stinging tentacles. *Rhizostoma pulmo* is a huge umbrella of jelly some two or three feet wide. Living, unharmed, inside the umbrella Montagu found tiny shrimps, *Hyperia galba*, which are usually restricted to this jellyfish. On occasions dolphins or porpoises are seen leaping, as in October 1991, and the most frequent, the bottle-nosed dolphin, was another of Montagu's discoveries.

On the rocks around the beaches are lichens. Above the reach of the sea are grey lichens, such as cudbear, black shields and sea ivory. Below them, in the splash zone are more orange lichens, *Caloplaca* species and *Xanthoria parietina*. Lower still is a tar black band of *Verrucaria maura*.

In the crannies and crevices of the splash zone, sea slaters and sea bristletails hide until dark and then scuttle over the rocks feeding on detritus. In similar cracks, exposed to the south-west, are small winkles, *Littorina neritoides*, clustered like pip-sized purple grapes. Rough winkles take over the same niche slightly lower down.

Where weeds cover the rock, they too are neatly zoned according to the length of time they are covered by the tides. Channel wrack, the stems grooved to speed the run-off of water, grows only near high water mark. Spiral wrack grows just below it and both harbour rough winkles. Below them is the wider zone of knotted wrack, sheltering well-camouflaged flat winkles and tufted with red *Polysiphonia* weed. Next comes the saw wrack, with serrated edges to the fronds.

Where wracks do not cover the rock, barnacles, those sedentary members of the crab family, sift the plankton when the tide is in, and limpets browse the algae. Feeding on these, and on the winkles, are the greyish-white dog whelks. This species has recovered after a catastrophic decline in the 80s, probably due to Tributyltin poisoning.

Sharp Tor from Sunny Cove

The wet sand between the tides is marked with the sandy tubes of sand mason worms and the coils of excrement from lugworms. Dig in the sand, and you will also find the silvery catworms, which wriggle like snakes when placed in water.

Growing from the sand, just below low water, is the large eel-grass *Zostera marina*. Long, green straps of a yard or so, and half an inch wide, wave as a forest beneath the waves. Chameleon prawns, pipefish and 15-spine sticklebacks are part of the community living within the forest. However, the eel-grass beds are small and vulnerable. They are easily damaged by boats grounding over them at low tide or by feet padding through them.

Over the rock ledges exposed at low tide there are a multitude of micro-habitats. In the gullies common winkles are clustered. On the bare rock, with barnacles and limpets, are thick top-shells and tussocks of fern-like *Laurencia pinnatifida* weed. Blobs of red jelly stuck to the rocks are beadlet anemones. The limp purple, green or beige tentacles splayed out in shallow water are snakelocks anemone. Lower and on the sides of the gullies carragheen mosses, *Chondrus crispus* and *Gigartina* species become common. Thin straps of seaweed, growing from a leathery button, are aptly named thong weed. Under these and the knotted and saw wracks are hidden breadcrumb sponges, grey and purple top shells, star ascidians and crabs. At the very lowest levels painted top shells, blue-rayed limpets and even cowries live on and under the oar weed forests. *Laminaria digitata*, the commonest oar weed, waves long-fingered hands extending some three metres. Long belts of the sugar kelp and the rare southern species *Laminaria ochroleuca* are mixed in the forest.

Scattered over and between the rocks are the rock pools. They are coated, as if with paint, by the purple rock weeds, *Lithophyllum* and *Lithothamnium* species. Pink 'trees' of corallina weed and green 'trees' of sea lettuce grow up from the sides. Long strands of Japweed and thong weed may lie on the surface. Amongst the weeds swim prawns, gobies, blennies and scorpion fish or fatherlashers. Under the stones lurk rocklings and butterfish, shorecrabs and the vicious, red-eyed fiddler or velvet swimming crab. Disturbance can kill these creatures and careful replacement of weed and stone is essential if we are not to impoverish this delicate world between the tides.

When all the people have left the rock pools and the sands, in the evening, it is easy to imagine Tennyson standing here, watching the ebb tide run out towards **The Bar** ...

'Sunset and evening star
And one clear call for me!
And may there be no moaning at the Bar
When I put out to sea,
But such a tide as moving seems asleep,
Too full for sound and foam,
When that which drew from out the boundless deep
Turns again home.'

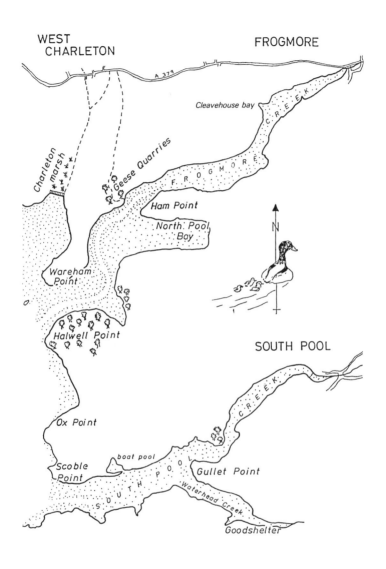

WEST
CHARLETON

FROGMORE

Cleavehouse bay

F R O G M O R E   C R E E K

Charleton marsh

Geese Quarries

Ham Point

North Pool
Bay

Wareham
Point

Halwell Point

SOUTH POOL

Ox Point

C R E E K

boat pool

Scoble
Point

Gullet Point

S O U T H   P O O L

Waterhead Creek

Goodshelter

N

A 379

FROGMORE and SOUTH POOL

0   ¼   1

approx.   miles

II

SOUTH POOL CREEK

Leaving **Salcombe** and **East Portlemouth** behind, three waterways open ahead. To the left is **Batson Creek**, straight ahead, between **Snapes** and **Scoble Points**, is the main channel north to **Kingsbridge** and to the right is **South Pool Creek**.

On the mud flats either side of the entrance to **South Pool Creek**, the first redshanks and curlew can be seen, feeding together with oystercatchers. These are our three most widespread waders. For most of the year there are about 200 of each on the estuary.

Redshank are quite small, brown waders, about 11 inches long, with whitish breasts and bellies. They walk jerkily on their bright orange legs, stabbing the mud for food. They take off noisily, repeating about three staccato notes. The white rump and white trailing edge to the wings are diagnostic. Their preferred food here seems to be ragworms, and they can sometimes be seen running down to the water's edge with a wriggling ragworm, to wash it in salty water before swallowing.

Greenshank and two redshank. Summer plumage

21

Curlew are large, brown waders, about 21 inches long, also with off-white underparts. They walk in a dignified way on long, grey legs. They will stop and peck at *Hydrobia* snails and small worms at or near the surface or insert their long, down-curved bill deep into the mud for lugworms or buried shellfish.

Shelduck also feed on the mud flats. They shuffle their red bills through the mud to sieve out the small *Hydrobia* snails. Shelduck look black and white at a distance but at closer range the beautiful chestnut band around the chest stands out.

On the northern bank is an old yacht basin, enclosed by a wall, with a narrow entrance. This section of **South Pool Creek**, in common with the lower part of all the creeks, has a rich fauna of sea squirts, peacock and other burrowing worms, shellfish, prawns and anemones. Shrimps, flounders and, in summer, grey mullet come in with the tide. In winter red-breasted mergansers fish here. The rich plankton brought in by the tide and the fauna of the mud support the fish and bird populations and it is important we do not destroy this apparently insignificant life by pollution or physical damage.

Gullet Point is attractively wooded with a mixture of pines and deciduous trees. This is where **Waterhead Creek** branches off to the right. On the rocks at the mouth of the creek, opposite **Gullet Point**, waders often gather as the rising tide forces them off the mud. Further up **Waterhead Creek** is the hamlet of **Goodshelter**, with a small boat yard where Alec Stone builds the famous Salcombe yawls.

The main channel of **South Pool Creek** snakes north-east, round **Quarry Plantation** on the left and the community of **Gullet Farm** on the right. At low water, waders congregate on the mud in the bay to the east of **Quarry Plantation**. This, and the rest of the creek up to **South Pool** village, is the best reach in which to see 'the queen of the waders', the greenshank. From July to March there are nearly always one or two, and sometimes up to 10.

Greenshank are slightly larger than redshank. They are startlingly white, especially in winter. They can almost be mistaken for gulls at a distance. Usually they feed like a redshank, stabbing at the mud but they also run through shallow water, pecking and threshing their bills from side to side. In flight, the long white wedge of the rump and lower back contrasts with the dark grey of the upper back and wings. Unlike the redshank, they have no white trailing edge to the wings. The call is haunting; a series of two to four drawn out notes, like a flute playing in a minor key. Sometimes the call is shorter and throatier.

Where the creek reaches the village, you can cross the narrow

Stepping stones at the head of the creek

stream by stepping stones or by the little road bridge. From the bridge, in the murky pool by the overhanging ash tree, you may see grey mullet and the opossum shrimps on which they feed.

Trying to walk along the foreshore is difficult. It is very muddy in places and you can get cut off by the tide. Walking also means disturbance to every bird on the creek.

South Pool itself is a picturesque village. The mediaeval church is beautiful. From the hedgerows around the village you can often hear the monotonous, rattling call of the cirl bunting. It is closely related to the yellowhammer and the song is similar but lacks the wheezing ' . . . no che-e-se' at the end. The female is like a female yellowhammer but without the rusty rump. The male has a striking yellow and black striped head, a black chin and yellow and green breast bands.

This is the bird that so excited George Montagu, when he was the first to find it in Britain. Perhaps it was here that he first saw one, for he certainly visited **South Pool**. An old man from the village, in Victorian times, told how Montagu would ride by on his horse, with several of his spaniel dogs following. He was, the old man said, 'a genial man, with a good word for everyone.'

Cirl buntings were found throughout most of England at the

Downstream from South Pool

beginning of this century but they have declined drastically. South Devon, where they were first discovered, now holds more than 90% of the British population. In winter, small flocks gather round the edges of fields to glean the weed seeds. One of the major reasons for decline is thought to be the lack of seeds, due to our more efficient weed control.

III

BATSON AND SNAPES POINT

Past **Salcombe** waterfront, **Whitestrand** and **Island Quays**, where swans and gulls squabble for scraps, you see the flotilla of yachts at their moorings. These and the marker posts and jetties provide attachment for seaweeds, mussels, sea squirts, anemones, brittle starfish and soft corals like 'dead men's fingers'. The weeds are often encrusted with colonies of sea firs. On the sides and bottoms of some of the big mooring pontoons there is a particularly rich collection, including jewel anemones, which do not occur anywhere else in the estuary. These thick growths can attract browsing fish. A friend recalls sleeping in his yacht and hearing a faint scraping on the bottom. He investigated and found a shoal of grey mullet gently mouthing at his weedy hull. Other noises are likely to be made by mute swans knocking for titbits.

Island Quay and Batson Creek from above Snapes Manor

At **Island Quay**, when the fishing boats are off-loading their catch, crowds of gulls gather. To the left is **Batson Creek**. A pair of swans is usually in residence and they sometimes nest along the less disturbed northern shore. There are two bays on this bank. A spur of rocks juts out from the side of one of them and on this, oystercatchers and redshank roost as the tide rises to cover the mud. The occasional greenshank joins them. On this side also there is a lime kiln. There are 22 kilns dotted around the estuary. From the middle of the 18th century until the end of the 19th they provided lime to spread on the fields as fertilizer, together with sea sand, dredged from **The Bar**, and sea weed. Boats brought limestone from Plymouth, the nearest quarry source, and this was tipped down into the conical kiln from the wide open top, with alternating layers of coal. When it was filled, a fire was lit at the bottom and, as the layers of coal slowly burned through, the limestone rock was turned to powder. The lime could then be taken by cart straight out onto the fields.

In May, and from July to September, up to about six common sandpipers may be seen along the shore. Sometimes a single bird will stay the winter. They are small, sandy-brown waders with short legs, white underparts and a brown crescent on the side of the breast. They have a characteristic habit of wagging their stumpy tails as they walk along the creekside. When they fly it is with a fast, direct flight, low over the water, propelled by stiff, quivering wings; then short glides on down-turned pinions. The high-pitched, trilling call carries far over the water, especially on calm evenings.

Along **Batson Creek** and round **Snapes Point** several cirl buntings hold territory and frequently sing from the scrubby elms that still survive.

Walking along the road that follows the northern shore towards **Snapes Manor** you will see two rare plants. They are both restricted to south-west Britain and the Kingsbridge area is their stronghold. The plants with big, arrow-shaped leaves are lords and ladies, or cuckoo pint, or parson in the pulpit, or hobblegobbles or Kittycome-downthelanejumpupandkissme — or whatever you want to call the wild arum *Arum maculatum*. Some of the plants have darker green leaves, with white or creamy veins instead of green ones. These plants are the rare cuckoo pint, *Arum italicum*; its leaves come up in October, nearly two months before those of common cuckoo pint. The flowers come out in May or June, about a month after the commoner plant. The spadix (the part of the flower looking like the erect parson in his pulpit) is always yellow in rare cuckoo pint. Common cuckoo pint sometimes has yellow (ladies) but usually purple (lords). Both are pollinated by small owl midges that are trapped overnight in the pollinating chambers below the 'parson'.

Arum italicum

The other rare plant is balm-leaved figwort, *Scrophularia scorodonia*. It is found on disturbed hedgebanks. It grows about five feet tall and has reddish-brown, fig-shaped flowers and oval leaves, wrinkled like the garden herb, balm. There are a number of insects associated with figworts. Wasps crawl into the flowers to obtain nectar and pollinate them. Fragments of what appear to be bird droppings resting on the leaves are really small figwort weevils. They are black, grey and white insects with a long, curved proboscis; antennae stick out at right angles from it, reminiscent of a pair of glasses on the end of an old gentleman's nose! Sometimes there are pale green caterpillars, speckled with black and yellow, on the leaves. These are the larvae of the mullein moth, which feed on any figwort and on the felty grey leaves of mullein.

Just short of **Snapes Manor**, a footpath is sign-posted up the valley to the left. It zig-zags up to a broad track that leads to **Snapes Point**. From this track is a fine view over **Batson Creek** to **Salcombe**. On a spring day ravens and buzzards can be seen performing acrobatics and soaring over the small conifer plantation. The gorse and thorn hedges on either side of the path have the star-like whorls of wild madder sprawling over them, while at the base of the hedges its common relatives, goosegrass and hedge bedstraw, abound − another good habitat for bloody-nosed beetles.

Where the signpost to **Snapes Point** diverts you from the main track, off to the left and over a stile, there is a lovely old pasture field. As well as five kinds of buttercup, there are spear, creeping, musk and

The Bag with mooring pontoons and behind the yachts, Egremont

seaside thistle all within a few yards of each other. There are bench
seats set in the field, by some gorse bushes, from which there are
glorious views down the estuary, over **Salcombe** to **Sharp Tor** and
the jagged rocks below it. To the left **South Pool Creek** stretches
away eastwards.

The path continues northwards, giving views across the estuary to
Egremont, an old Mersey ferry, now serving retirement as the floating
headquarters of the Island Cruising Club. The club runs a variety of
courses for all ages and stages of mariner. They own wind-surfers,
small yachts and large yachts including the elegant Edwardian
schooner *Hoshi* and the sturdy ex-Brixham trawler *Provident*. In the
old trees behind *Egremont*, a few pairs of herons may nest. Several
patrol the water's edge on either side of **The Bag**, as this section
between **Snapes Point** and **Heath Point** is called. When the tide is
in they may stand incongruously in the fields south of **Halwell Wood**;
more than 20 have been seen together here.

The path slopes down to a stand of wych elms along the shore line.
Growing from the cliff top are also oaks, blackthorn and hawthorn
scrub and patches of spindleberry bushes, which can be recognised,
even in mid-winter, by their green twigs. In autumn the pink and
orange berries are a picture. In spring and early summer chiffchaffs,
willow warblers and blackcaps join the resident robins, proclaiming
their territories, particularly where the strip of scrub widens out into
woodland around **Tosnos Point**. At migration times the cliff top

corridor provides cover and feeding for warblers as they pass through.

On the near side of the muddy bay are the remains of several old boats. This 'graveyard' provides roosting places for gulls and redshank at high water. Along the collapsing skeleton of a former J class yacht dozens of redshank may crowd in line. Out on the buoys and pontoons more gulls, cormorants and a few sandwich terns perch.

As the path veers left, after **Tosnos Point**, a new forest of masts comes into view at **Lincombe** boatyard. The mud flats off **Lincombe** are some of the first to be exposed as the tide falls. As soon as they appear, curlew, redshank and oystercatcher fly in from their high tide roosts and begin to feed.

By **Lincombe** the path climbs steeply to reveal a wonderful panoramic view of the estuary, stretching from **Kingsbridge** to the west, past **Bowcombe**, **Charleton** marsh and village, **Wareham Point** and **Frogmore Creek** to the village of **Frogmore** to the east. Just off **Wareham Point** is the **Saltstone**. Except at high tide, a tonsure of dark seaweed is visible round the island's yellowish shingle pate.

Shortly after this breathtaking view, you reach the National Trust car park. The circular walk that can start and finish here gives views from the mouth to the head of the estuary; an exhilarating way to gain an impression of the whole estuary in less than an hour.

Common sandpiper

IV

FROGMORE CREEK

Turning east from **Halwell Point**, you enter **Frogmore Creek**, leaving the **Saltstone** and **Wareham Point** on your left. Frogmore is the most extensive creek of the estuary; more than two miles long. On your right is **Halwell Wood**. It gives an idea of what the rolling slopes, dipping down to the estuary, looked like before the natural woodland was cleared. In the small copse on the eastern side of **Halwell Bay** is the main heronry. About five pairs nest, usually in the tall scots pines. They start building in February and by the end of April they are feeding the large young, which can be seen exercising their wings. When the young birds have fledged, they stand by the water's edge learning to fish, like their parents. They are without the black plumes of the adults and their appearance is rather untidy.

Frogmore Creek to the right and Charleton Bay to the left,
viewed from above Lincombe boatyard

Herons are masters of the waiting game; an example to all human anglers. They will wait, still as a statue, beak pointed down, ready to strike, or pointed upwards, when the whole bird resembles a bleached post, sticking out of the mud at a drunken angle. Then a sudden stride forward, the dagger bill lunges and is withdrawn from the water gripping a flounder or an eel. You can see eels writhing their bodies around the heron's neck in a vain effort to escape. Finally it will be swallowed, in gulps, whole.

For hours after a meal, herons attend to their toilet. They have patches of powder down on their lower breast and on their thighs, so they can simultaneously rub powder onto their head and neck. When the slime from their wrigglesome meal has been well coated with powder, they use their middle toe, which is flattened and pectinated, as a comb to comb out powder and slime together.

On the northern bank of the creek, opposite **Halwell Wood**, are thickets of blackthorn and some fine oak trees. Being so well sheltered from the prevailing, salt-laden westerly winds and from the cold northerly ones, the oak leaves and catkins are out by the middle of April, a week or more earlier than most. In the friable cliff below, rabbits and badgers burrow and make their runs. On the rocks are lichens, thrift, sea campion, rock spurrey, sea plantain and rock samphire. These occur on most of the rocky cliffs all round the estuary. Similarly there is a typical community of plants growing just above high water mark, at the base of the cliff. The most frequent species are sea beet, corn sow-thistle, sea couch grass and halberd-leaved orache. It is from sea beet, cultivated since the time of the ancient Egyptians, that we have developed our cultivated varieties of beetroot, spinach and sugar beet. Landslips from the cliffs produce a disturbed soil where balm-leaved figwort and stinking iris grow.

Where the northern bank of the creek turns sharply to the left, there is a spit of small, slatey fragments built up by the waves and current. It is always changing shape, depending on wind strength and direction and the height of the tides. Just before the spit the crinkled and contorted shells of Pacific oysters may be washed up. These are from the cultivation cages laid down in the bottom of the creek leading into **North Pool Bay** and from **Charleton Creek**. The oyster fishery ceased in the mid-eighties; the poor results probably caused by Tributyltin contamination.

From this spit, one September, an osprey was seen. It gave a splendid display of plunge diving. Five times it rose clumsily from the estuary and shook the water from its feathers in a halo of spray, but with its talons empty. The sixth time it rose triumphant with a grey mullet clasped like a silver torpedo. Ospreys may pass through on migration in most years.

31

Osprey with thick-lipped Grey Mullet

At very low water, a population of peacock and other burrowing worms, sponges and sea squirts is revealed here. This and the diving birds that frequent this part of the creek are indicative of the richness of the underwater fauna. The main channel from the spit to **Geese Quarry Wood** is the principal feeding area of the diving duck that use the estuary in winter. There are up to 50 goldeneye in a hard winter. Pochard, which seem to be increasing, may join them. Red-breasted mergansers, great crested and little grebes all favour this curve of the channel.

To the east is the wide, shallow bay of **North Pool**. This is a prime area of mud-flat, covered with green patches of *Enteromorpha* weed and rich in worms and shellfish. The peppery furrow shell is the commonest bivalve but carpet shells, the big sand gapers and cockles are frequent. As soon as the mud is exposed, in fly the curlew, oystercatcher and redshank. The redshank prefer the edge of the ribbon of water that threads its way across the bay. The curlew are mostly on the higher, central area of mud. The shillety shore along **Ham Point** attracts more oystercatchers. At the far end of the bay lapwing sometimes congregate, especially in autumn or during a cold spell in winter. Throughout the winter, several hundred wigeon feed on the *Enteromorpha* at the head and edges of the bay. Shelduck loaf and feed on the mud and in spring the males display, raising their bills and making aggressive whickering cries and grunts. A pair usually nest on **Ham Point** promontary in one of the many old rabbit burrows.

Geese Quarry may have been the quarry from which slate was shipped to **Dartmouth**, in the reign of Henry VIII, to help build Dartmouth Castle. Now it supports a pleasant little wood. After many of its trees died, due to Dutch elm disease, the owner replanted, mainly with oaks. There is a path that winds up through the wood and over to **West Charleton**.

Soon after **Geese Quarry Wood**, along the foreshore, another path leads up and follows the low cliff top all the way to **Frogmore** village. After nearly a mile, the path and creek turn north-west. Opposite here, on the southern bank, is a bay where about six greenshank may be seen at almost any time of the year. In autumn there are sometimes more than 20.

Before **Cleavehouse Bay** there are some lovely early purple orchids. In April and May the purple flowers are out in spikes more than a foot tall. Where the path comes down to shore level at **Cleavehouse Bay**, there is an attractive little saltmarsh. It has a turf of the saltmarsh grass *Puccinellia maritima*, with patches of sea plantain, sea arrow-

Early purple orchids (*Orchis mascula*)

grass, sea milkwort and sea aster. At its upper edge there is a saltmarsh sedge *Carex extensa*, which can always be identified by its long bracts below the flower heads, and sea club-rush, which tends to grow where fresh water seeps down to the shore. A pair of swans attempt to breed near here in most years.

On both sides of the creek are old lime kilns and it is interesting to see how many of them have old man's beard growing nearby. It is a plant that usually indicates a limey soil.

The last section of the creek often provides a flurry of interest. There is a shingle spit jutting out from the southern bank. This attracts a small, wintering flock of dunlin, with a few ringed plover and perhaps a common sandpiper in attendance. When the tide is high, oystercatchers and even redshanks feed on the pasture fields beside the creek on its southern side. A greenshank or two often wades up and down the main channel and sometimes comes right up to the bridge that spans the top of the creek. At high water, dunlin and grey plover sometimes fly up **Frogmore Creek** to roost on the shingle at **Slapton** beach and, as the tide begins to fall they return.

Flocks of gulls feed in the central channel. From March to July the black-headed gulls are away at their breeding haunts on the coastal marshes of Hampshire, Sussex and Kent. Then they come flooding back, their dark brown heads already changing to the 'winter' plumage of white, with a dark smudge behind the eye. Although so common, they are beautiful birds. The pale grey of the wings contrasts with their pure white leading edges, and red legs and red bill give a dash of colour. Some herring gulls remain during the summer. In fact their numbers increase in February and March, as birds wintering elsewhere return to our south Devon cliffs to nest.

When the winter storms blow, gulls fly down Frogmore valley from **Start Bay**, to shelter in the estuary. A stream of great black-backed gulls, herring gulls and some over-wintering lesser black-backs will fly westwards; the total number can be more than a thousand.

Right at the head of the creek is a tussocky patch of sedge, growing a yard tall, and identified by Ray Gould, a local naturalist, as the rare galingale.

V

BLANKSMILL AND COLLAPIT CREEKS

The wide tidal area between **Rowden** and **Wareham Points** is locally known as **Widegates**. The western side is formed by the joint mouth of the two creeks, **Blanksmill** and **Collapit**. In the winter, red-breasted mergansers fish where the creeks join the main estuary channel.

Hundreds of wigeon also gather here and, as the tide rises, drift up the creeks. There may be a few dozen teal with them. In a normal winter they start arriving in October and by December and January there are about 1,000 wigeon and 200 teal on the estuary. In the 1960s, when Ronald Price of Charleton counted the wildfowl, these numbers were twice as high. These duck are easily disturbed by walkers, wildfowlers, fishermen or birdwatchers. By March virtually all of them will have returned to their breeding grounds, as far away as Eastern Europe.

The teal are concentrated on the western side of the estuary, especially from **Collapit Creek** to **Park Bay**. They dabble in the runnels that snake through the mudflats and look for small worms, crustaceans and molluscs, scraps of weed and seeds; a catholic diet. Teal are noticeably smaller than wigeon. The duck is brown and the drake is greyish with a dark head and a triangular, cream patch by his tail. When seen closely the head is deep red with a wide, green eye-stripe edged in cream. When they fly, both sexes show a white line across the inner part of the wing.

Female wigeon have brown upperparts and a white belly. The drakes have striking plumage − a red-brown head, a yellow stripe down the forehead, grey bill, pink breast, pale grey back, black tail and a white patch in front of the tail. In flight the drakes show distinctive white shoulder patches. Their call is a high whistle, quite unlike the familiar mallard's quacking. When the incoming tide covers the mudflats wigeon flocks may fly up to graze on pasture or winter cereals. At low water they graze on the *Zostera angustifolia* and *Enteromorpha*, which grow on the mudflats.

As the tide rises, the wintering flock of dark-breasted brent geese often gathers by **Gerston Point**. The flock has increased from only

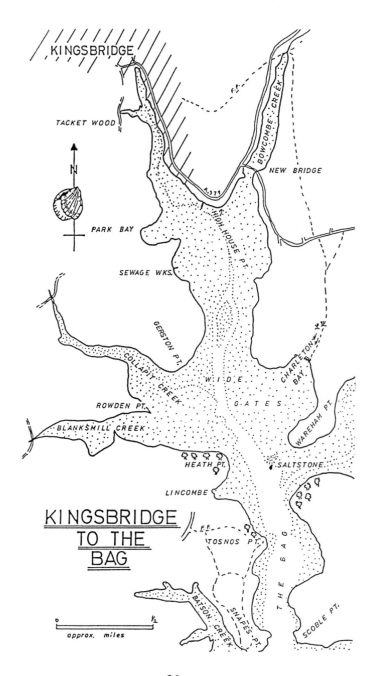

KINGSBRIDGE

TACKET WOOD

PARK BAY

N

SEWAGE WKS.

BOWCOMBE CREEK

NEW BRIDGE

A.379

HIGH HOUSE PT.

GERSTON PT.

COLLAPIT CREEK

CHARLETON BAY

WIDE

GATES

WAREHAM PT.

ROWDEN PT.

BLANKSMILL CREEK

HEATH PT.

SALTSTONE

LINCOMBE

KINGSBRIDGE
TO THE
BAG

F.P.

TOSNOS PT.

T H E   B A G

BATSON CREEK

SNAPES PT.

SCOBLE PT.

0   ½
approx. miles

36

Curlew, Oystercatcher and a Grey Plover

one in 1978 to about 60 in the early '90s. In the hard winter of January 1982, 250 white fronted geese spent a fortnight grazing the huge field of winter wheat above **Rowden Point**. Eleven were shot. It is interesting that, on the day that they left a party of similar size was seen arriving at Slimbridge. During the same cold snap there were six barnacle geese on the estuary.

During the last two years numbers of Canada geese have increased locally and two or three dozen frequently fly in to the fields by **Gerston Point** at dusk. They make a romantic sound and silhouette against a sunset sky.

On the large area of mudflats between **Gerston** and **Heath Points**, waders feed; a hundred or more curlew on the higher parts, with redshank, mainly along the creeks and runnels, and oystercatchers closest in to **Gerston** and **Rowden Points**. It is a major site for grey plover. More than 20 may be spread out, keeping to territories, until they flock together as the tide covers the mud. Even in winter plumage they are easy to recognise; a little larger and plumper than a redshank, with a typical way of patrolling their patch of mud. They take a few steps forward and then pause, looking for signs of potential prey on or under the mud, ... a few more steps, pause ... and so on. If the redshank is the most neurotic of waders to anthropomorphic eyes, then the grey plover is the most phlegmatic. When it flies, it reveals black patches under the wings; the only wader to have black 'arm-pits'. Its cry is a double note falling in pitch, giving an impression of sadness.

Several hundred dunlin, sometimes up to a thousand, flock along the edge of the creeks or main channel, or spread across the expanse of mud. They will suddenly take off, stirred by the appearance of a peregrine, a motor boat, or for no apparent reason. Starling like, the flock of hundreds will fly as a single unit, twisting to reveal

The narrow and sinuous Collapit Creek

hundreds of white bellies at the same instant and twisting again to become almost invisible against the grey-brown mud.

At high water, many of the waders roost on the shingle and rock of **Rowden** and **Gerston Points**. The oystercatchers, along with gulls and cormorants, often choose the shingle spits that extend from both banks of **Blanksmill Creek** for their high tide roosts. Small groups of greenshank favour the bay on the Collapit side of **Rowden Point**. In August of 1989, six little egrets regularly roosted in the dead elms above this bay, with about the same number of grey herons, in perfect amity. It is tempting to think they may nest with the herons some day for several birds have been seen since. We live in hope; little egrets have been spreading and now breed in Brittany.

From July to March, as dusk approaches, several thousand black-headed gulls fly down all the creeks and valleys, from the fields where they have been feeding by day, to roost in **Widegates**. On a sunny evening you could be watching a flypast of flamingoes, for the sunset glow gives them a delicate pink flush.

The main rook and jackdaw roost in the southern part of the **South Hams** is often in the woods at **Heath Point** or **Halwell** but you need to stay until almost dark for their arrival. Hundreds of birds, 'cawing and jacking', stream into the black woods and rise into the darkening sky before fluttering back into the woods like black snowflakes.

The wide funnel of **Blanksmill Creek** is very shallow. The edge is topped by thorn scrub, elm suckers and a few stunted oaks. The fields rise gently either side. Of all the creeks Blanksmill is the most windswept and exposed. In April, the blackthorns all round the estuary give an impressive display of 'blackthorn winter'. In Blanksmill it is perhaps most impressive, with the wind whipping the petals from the bushes and sending them scudding over the creek like real snowflakes.

On the northern bank is a fine lime kiln. The main channel winds in great loops across the whole width of the creek and on some of the bends empty shells show up as white stippling.

Shelduck, gulls and redshanks are the main species at low water, with a few greenshank, particularly up near Blanksmill bridge. If you wait in a car at **Blanksmill bridge**, as the tide is rising, you may have wonderful views, not only of these species but of the wigeon, floating ever closer. If you emerge from the car they will immediately take flight and within a minute the creek will be empty. Both creeks are all too easily disturbed.

The head of the creek has a small saltmarsh, with tall sea couch grass on the bank and saltmarsh grass and sea aster below. The sea aster is a picture in pale purple at michaelmas daisy time. Sea club-rush and saltmarsh sedge grow here and in patches along both banks. The classic flowering plant that first colonises firm mud, glasswort, is also in evidence. A succulent little plant some six inches high, it is like a cactus without the prickles. Annual seablight, a similar but tougher, more glaucous species, grows above it.

Collapit Creek is much narrower and more serpentine. It is sheltered by steep slopes and so has fine, flourishing oaks along its banks, but it is completely unsuitable for walking. It has very soft mud right up to the edge of the creek. But through the gateways, along the lane between the heads of the two creeks, are some attractive views of **Collapit**. From the bridge over the stream leading into the creek you see another fringe of saltmarsh. Beyond it, on the mud, will be a greenshank, a few redshank, a pair or two of shelduck and perhaps a little egret, if you are lucky; in which case you may also see a sudden flash of blue and hear a sharp whistle, which is the closest experience that most of us get of a kingfisher.

Kingfisher with goby

39

VI

CHARLETON BAY AND MARSH

Cormorants on Saltstone

At the entrance to **Charleton Bay** is the **Saltstone**, a rock and shingle island, covered at high water. On the shingle crest, cormorants gather, to spread and dry their wings after fishing. Fancifully, they resemble the non-conformist ministers, like John Hicks and John Flavell, in black cassocks, addressing their congregations here in the 17th century; an island retreat out of the jurisdiction of persecuting magistrates like Beare of **Bearscombe**. Anne Born, in her *History of Kingsbridge and Salcombe* gives a detailed account of those times.

The **Saltstone** was one of the favourite hunting grounds of George Montagu. About 20 of the species of worm, crustacea or mollusc that he found there are still present although, perhaps, in reduced numbers. They are described in his *Testacea Britannica* and illustrated by his mistress, Eliza, with carefully coloured etchings.

When the Marine Biological Association made its first full survey of an estuary in 1900, it chose Montagu's **Kingsbridge Estuary**. They found most of the species that he recorded and some new ones, such

Spiny Starfish

as a single specimen of the spiny starfish *Marthasterias glacialis*. I found a single specimen in exactly the same position 85 years later. Since about 1980, Japweed, the introduced and invasive *Sargassum muticum*, its trailing fronds berried with all too efficient 'fruiting' bodies, has become established at low water to the south of the **Saltstone**.

C. M. Yonge's classic book, *The Sea-shore*, has six plates taken near the **Saltstone** and its opening quotation is from Montagu. Universities and the Field Studies Centre at Slapton have voluntarily stopped taking parties to the **Saltstone**, in an effort to avoid damaging the fragile habitat. Please respect this very special place and leave it undisturbed.

At low water you can enjoy a view of some of the species Montagu saw by walking down over the seaweeds from **Wareham Point** to the edge of the mud by **Frogmore Creek** rather than going to the **Saltstone**. On the fronds of knotted and saw wracks are sea firs, or hydroids. Many of them look like little grey trees, less than an inch high. Some are globules of pink jelly stuck to the wracks. Under the wracks and stones may be butterfish, crabs, brittlestars, sea squirts, anemones and sea urchins. The urchins camouflage themselves with scraps of weed. Attached to stones or the bases of weed are greyish, leathery bags an inch or two long. These are sea squirts, mostly *Ascidiella aspersa*. Out on the mud, near low water mark, grow pinnacled patches of orange sponge, *Hymeniacidon perleve*.

Where water runs over the gravelly mud, old winkle and whelk shells often have hermit crabs living inside them. Some shells are covered in spiky fur, which is another hydroid, *Hydractinia echinata*.

On a very low tide forests of pencil-like tubes stick out of the mud. These belong to peacock worms, which spread their feathery tentacles, as a peacock spreads its tail, to catch plankton. Another tube worm, *Myxicola infundibulum*, has a brown fan spreading from a slimy tube

41

just proud of the mud.

These are just a few of the creatures Montagu found, nearly 200 years ago, on and around the **Saltstone**.

On our monthly counts of estuary birds Bryan Ashby and I often stop for refreshment at **Wareham Point**. Between November and February we may see a great northern diver, fishing in the deep water channel to the south and west of the **Saltstone**. In some years at least four are seen together. As we scan for waders, wildfowl and the great northern diver, a robin waits in the thorn scrub behind us. One of us lifts some of the rotting weed along high tide mark. Side-shrimps leap up in alarm and, as we sip our coffee and nibble biscuits, the robin hops down to join us for elevenses.

Broken whelk shells were littered on the stony shore at **Wareham Point**. Herring gulls picked up large whelk shells, inhabited by hermit crabs, from near low tide mark, then flew up and dropped them on the stones. Niko Tinbergen, in his study of the herring gull, considered that they dropped shells at random. However, the herring gulls in New Jersey, USA, regularly used a road bridge on which to drop clams to break them. So perhaps the gulls of Kingsbridge and New Jersey shared an exceptionally high IQ? Recently there have been no new broken shells. Are the educational standards of our herring gulls falling?!

On the eastern side of **Charleton Bay** cart tracks are worn into the soft Devon slate. They were made before the last world war by carts collecting seaweed and shellfish. Even the central rut formed by the patient plodding of the horse still remains.

The low cliff above the shore is a jumbled mass of flakey fragments. This is, in geologists' jargon, 'head'. Each spring, towards the end of the latest ice age some 10,000 years ago, landslip material slid like larva over the permanently frozen sub-soil. Here in the head the swirling movement is preserved. Although southern England was never covered by glaciers, it did have tundra conditions and it was during that time that populations of waders and wildfowl became separated and the present day sub-species and migration patterns developed. A good example is the dunlin, which is discussed later.

The low trees and bushes above the cliff, which look as if they have been cut with a hedge-trimmer, are wind-pruned by the salty, south-west winds. Among the predominant thorns a group of pear trees survives, their big, white blossoms and glassy green leaves incongruous in this windswept spot. Only 100 yards to the east, sheltered from the wind, the early oaks on **Frogmore Creek** flourish like bubbling green cumulous clouds.

Because it faces south-west, **Charleton Bay** is the resting place of much of the flotsam and jetsam driven by the prevailing wind. Along the tideline are the oval, white 'bones' that formed the internal skeletons of cuttlefish, and clusters of papery bubbles in which young whelks have hatched, eaten their siblings and floated, bloated, into the plankton. 'Mermaids' purses', the egg-cases of dogfish and rays, are common. Those which have tendrils at the four corners belong to dogfish. Those with points belong to rays. Thornback ray cases are the more common; about three inches long, with all four points about equal in size. A similar sized case, with one pair of points twice as long as the other and spreading apart, belongs to the spotted ray *Raja montagui*, named after George Montagu.

The bay also collects man's rubbish which, until recently, made the head of the bay a plastic-strewn eyesore. Thanks to a few dedicated local people collecting the litter and the farmer taking the collected rubbish to the local tip, the problem is kept contained.

When, a few years ago, it was proposed to site a marina in **Charleton Marsh** and dig a deep-water channel across the bay, I carried out a study of the ecology of **Charleton Bay**. After mapping and recording was completed, attempts were made to correlate the distribution of the feeding birds with the distribution of the invertebrate life.

The weed-covered, rocky shores on both sides of the bay proved an important high-water roost for waders from all over the estuary, particularly during autumn migration. There is desultory feeding, presumably on rough winkles, *Hydrobia* snails, side-shrimps and small shore-crabs present in the channel and spiral wrack zones. At low water the only birds using this habitat are turnstones and over-wintering rock pipits. All the others are using different parts of the muddy bay.

Dunlin had a very strong correlation with the small tube-worm, *Melinna palmata*, and the *Hydrobia* snails, when they were considered together. Both can be easily reached by the dunlins' short bills. Most dunlin feed on the plateaux or the slopes leading down to low water, particularly the western side, near the main channel.

Dunlin are the most abundant waders both here and in Britain as a whole. Three sub-species visit the estuary. Ringing recoveries have shown that in April and May the birds are *Calidris alpina schinzii*, migrating north to the moorlands of northern Britain or Iceland, or *Calidris alpina arctica* bound for Greenland; both winter down to the north-west coast of Africa. The return passage of *Calidris alpina schinzii* and *arctica* begins in mid-June and continues until the end of September. In October *Calidris alpina alpina*, which breed in Scandinavia and Russia, begin to arrive on the estuary and build up until in February and March they return.

There was no clear correlation with any species or group of species for curlew. They were seen to take *Hydrobia* snails, pecked from the surface, and big lugworms from deep in the mud, mostly from the south and west of the plateaux.

Oystercatchers' distribution was correlated, very significantly, with the distribution of cockles, which were most common in the sandier, southern section of the bay. The adults' blunt-ended bill has no nerve endings and has the power to crack the thick shells. Where no cockles were recorded, there were fewest oystercatchers. Goss-Custard (1983) found that first year birds on the Exe often specialise in worms and then transfer to cockles or mussels in their second year. However he also found a few remained worm specialists and a few became winkle specialists, complete with a curved tip to the bill as a result of much winkle picking! This is probably also true on the **Kingsbridge Estuary**. Several of those seen feeding where ragworms were common were young birds, having pointed, dark-tipped bills. Although concentrated where cockles were abundant, oystercatchers showed a more even spread over the whole mudflat than the other waders, with the exception of grey plover. Goss-Custard found that colour-ringed birds returned to the same section of mudflat each winter. These winter territories are not strictly adhered to, but probably ensure a fairly even distribution with a bias to the areas rich in cockles.

There was a clear correlation between the distribution of redshank and that of ragworms. Both were commonest at the head of the bay and down the sides of the creek channel. On the extensive plateaux of the mudflats, they sometimes peck in the pools, perhaps capturing shrimps or fish fry.

Greenshanks, when they peck and probe like redshanks, may also be feeding on ragworms. When they run through the water in the creek or make darting stabs into the pools on the plateaux, shrimps and small fish are probably the prey.

Grey plovers show some preference for the edge of the western plateau and the slope, from it, down to the main channel. Worms are the most frequent invertebrates here, especially *Melinna palmata*, which has a correlation with grey plover but not at a significant level. Montagu recorded *Melinna* in **Charleton Bay**, 'like bits of straw covered with mud, and as close and numerous as stubble in a field.' It is still common and recognisable by the limp cream tentacles sticking out at an angle from the tube. The plover are also correlated with *Capitellid* worms; reddish worms with swollen ends and living in spiralling burrows. But, like the oystercatcher, the grey plover is spread fairly evenly. This fits in with Jim Flegg's discovery (1985) that grey plover are remarkably faithful to their winter territories, returning year after year to the same few square yards of mud.

In the 1970s up to 1,000 golden plover used to rest on the plateau areas of **Charleton Bay** and the other main mudflats. They made spectacular flights over the estuary. Since then their visits have become infrequent and numbers have fallen. Today a hundred or two is a good-sized flock.

Bar-tailed godwits favour the mud at the water's edge, jabbing with their slightly up-tilted bill, or moving it up and down like a sewing machine. This method loosens the mud and makes it easier to pull the worms from their burrows. About a dozen usually winter on the estuary. Occasionally, flocks of more than a hundred pass through on spring passage, as in 1984 and 1990, when many were in their fine chestnut-breasted summer plumage.

Herons wrestle with eels or peck at smaller fry in the plateau pools. There is often a heron around the **Saltstone** and another along the upper creek, near the sluice exit from **Charleton Marsh**. At high water they fly over into the marsh itself.

In 1805, the Lord of the Manor of Charleton, Lord Boringdon, had French prisoners of war construct a sea wall to cut off the upper part of **Charleton Creek**, with a view to making it agriculturally productive. Some crops have been grown and at one stage it was used as a rifle range but to a greater or lesser extent it has always remained marshy. Its potential as a marshland nature reserve is mouth-watering.

Heron on West Charleton Marsh

45

Thick-lipped Grey Mullet

Inside the wall is a wide ditch, which is connected to the bay outside by the sluice. The effectiveness of the sluice is variable, and from time to time salt water enters the marsh, along with grey mullet. Mick Loates has noted that these fish usually arrive in late April and May; both fry, from about two inches long, and mature fish of up to 18 inches. The juveniles, especially, swim in shoals, darting to and fro, making the water swirl and showing their silver sides as they turn. Opossum shrimps too enter through the sluice in vast numbers. There is a resident kingfisher which sits on the sluice gates and takes his pick.

Three narrow ditches lead from the main ditch and drain the 40 acre marsh. When they are dredged out, the spoil contains shells, mostly peppery furrow shells, which would have been living in the tidal flats when Montagu was walking down **Charleton Creek** to visit the **Saltstone**. There are three areas of reed-bed, which may be surrounded by a meadow of sea club-rush. When the sluice is faulty and is flooding the marsh with salt water each high tide, the club-rush decreases and there is more bare mud. The sea club-rush provides nesting sites for reed buntings. In the reed-beds are a few pairs of reed warbler. They build their deep, cup-shaped nests round several reed stems, about three feet above the level of the water. The nest is so deep that the four eggs do not fall out, even when the whispering reeds are bent almost double by a fierce wind. However, cuckoos often lay in reed warblers' nests and then eggs and young will be humped over the side by the all-demanding chick.

Several plants which are restricted to brackish conditions grow in the wetter parts; celery-leaved buttercup, whose leaves live up to its name, and two uncommon saltmarsh grasses – *Puccinellia rupestris* and *Puccinellia distans*.

In the spring and autumn, rare migrants can be seen on **Charleton**

Marsh. Spoonbills, little egrets and great white egret and an osprey have all visited in the last five years, as well as some exotic escapes such as ruddy shelduck, sacred ibis and a pair of white storks from Whipsnade Zoo!

In February and March, lesser black-backed gulls, returning from Africa, rest on the marsh, their yellow legs and slate-grey backs showing up against the green grass. A month later the whimbrels' vibrato calls echo overhead as they migrate northwards.

During the winter, duck fly in at dusk and stay until disturbed by early morning walkers, birdwatchers or wildfowlers. Teal, wigeon and small numbers of shoveler and pintail are attracted by the shallow pools among the tussocky grass. Mallard are present all through the year and, from early April, flotillas of duckings paddle furiously down the ditches and into the reeds. Shelduck use the marsh as a loafing area, particularly at high tide, and so do curlew and a few redshank, dunlin and greenshank. It is worth scanning the bare patches for other waders. Ruff, green and wood sandpipers, black-tailed godwit, spotted redshank, little stint, curlew sandpiper, ringed plover and little ringed plover have all been seen here. On one day, in the autumn of 1986, there were 32 ruff, some still in summer plumage, resting on the marsh. Montagu kept several ruff for up to four years and found the so-called greenwich sandpipers were merely ruff in winter plumage. In winter, near the reed beds, 20 or more common snipe and the occasional jack snipe are resident, probing their long bills into the soft mud.

On the wet grassland at the top of the marsh, a few water pipits usually winter. They are a rare and difficult species to identify. Beware, meadow pipits also winter here!

The rough grassland that stretches up from the reed-beds contains yellow iris, some marsh orchids, and plenty of ladies smock (or cuckoo flower), on which the orange-tip butterflies lay their eggs.

In the scrub and trees that fringe the marsh are the common hedgerow birds and, in summer, chiffchaff, willow warbler and whitethroat. At least one pair of lesser whitethroats also nest each year. The male has a rattling song, similar to the cirl bunting, which sometimes holds a territory. The hawthorn berries in the autumn attract parties of redwing and fieldfare.

At the top of the marsh is a lake, originally made to irrigate a nearby pick-your-own enterprise. It supports a few tufted duck in the winter, mallard and the occasional moorhen. Moorhens have decreased on the marsh with the increase of the predatory mink. Over the lake, a carpet of water fern spreads in the summer. Early and late swallows, martins and swifts hawk for insects above the marsh, lake and small sewage works.

Charleton Marsh

The sewage works is next to the lake, screened by evergreens. It is always worth looking along the trees and over the filter bed for birds. Greenfinches, goldfinches and collared doves are common in the trees and chaffinches, starlings and pied and grey wagtails feed on the filter-bed. Chiffchaffs feed on the filter-bed when they arrive in March and, one year, more than a dozen wintered. A sparrowhawk pays regular, unexpected visits. Perhaps this malodorous, sheltered oasis will, some day, produce a real rarity. Who will find the first hoopoe or red-breasted flycatcher?

VII

GERSTON POINT TO KINGSBRIDGE

Where the estuary narrows, between **Gerston** and **Charleton Points**, cormorants, and in winter time goldeneyes, red-breasted mergansers, a few great crested grebes and occasional Slavonian or black-necked grebe, scoter or long-tailed duck are busy diving. As the tide ebbs, a muddy shoal − **The Saddle** − appears in the middle of the main channel. It always attracts an interesting mixture of waders, shelduck and wigeon. The long-legged curlew are first to fly in from their high tide roosts in the fields to either side. Then follow redshank, a few grey plover, oystercatchers and perhaps a flock of dunlin.

On the west bank, north of **Gerston Point**, there used to be a duck decoy and the reedy area behind a stone wall is still called **Coypool**. Sarah Prideaux Fox records that it was 'much used for wild fowl' at the beginning of the 18th century.

Past some wych elms is a bay, backed by a modern sewage works, constructed in the 1970s. Before the works were built raw sewage from Kingsbridge flowed out near **High House Point** and every winter a flock of about 100 coot gathered round it. From the year the outflow ceased, the flock declined and within four years the coot had become a rare bird on the estuary.

The nutrients in the stream flowing out from the new treatment works have encouraged a luxuriant growth of *Enteromorpha* over the bay. Gulls flock round the works and redshank, wigeon and shelduck assemble in the bay. In the deep runnels curving through the mud, teal join the wigeon.

North of the sewage works bay lies **Park Bay**. The rocky promontories at each side of the bay are favourite roosting places for waders. As the tide rises and the mud is covered waders fly in, particularly to the northern promontory and the rocky islet offshore. As more fly in, they pack closer and closer together. The orange-red legs of the redshank are visible from a long way away and any greenshanks among them show up by their whiteness. This is where an avocet has been seen in early spring, on several occasions. Individuals from the wintering flock on the Tamar possibly call in on their way back to breed in Suffolk or Holland.

Wigeon

Park Bay can have three or four hundred wigeon and perhaps 100 teal and shelduck in winter. By autumn the resident flock of mallard can also be about 100. The duck float in the middle or are strung out along the edges and head of the bay. At the head is a dense growth of sea club-rush in which a pair of swans sometimes nest.

The wide mudflats that stretch out from **Park Bay** to **High House Point** and southwards to **Gerston** are, like **Charleton Bay**, a major feeding area for the waders and wildfowl and another loafing area for gulls. The best view of the mudflats and of **Park Bay** is from **Embankment Road** on the east bank. You can stand on the tarmac path or sit on the seats below and, with a pair of binoculars or a telescope, have a grandstand view. If you happen to be there when the tide begins to flood you may see the bore, a wall of water several inches high, moving steadily up the channel.

Towards **Kingsbridge** the creek narrows, buildings and the main road come right down to the water's edge and yet there is still wildlife interest. Sitting outside the Crabshell pub at high water, opposite the small but attractive **Tacket Wood Creek**, you can feed your crumbs to the gulls, mallards and swans that come begging, although they would be healthier on their natural diet. Swans, for reasons that are not clear, have decreased from about 80 on the estuary in the early 1960s to about 20 now. At low water redshank and greenshank feed by the thin trickle of water that still flows down the creek. In the winter

Kingsbridge Quay and the town beyond

small flocks of dunlin join them. Early in the morning, on a rising tide, red-breasted mergansers may come up this far.

The road and footpath follow the final few hundred yards of the creek towards the public conveniences. There can still be surprises. Mallard and gulls will swim and fly, flocking down to thrown-out scraps. Most of the gulls are black-headed but occasionally there is a Mediterranean black-headed gull among them. The slate wall beside the path has a good covering of lichens, especially the grey, warty patches of cudbear. Out of the wall grow tufts of rock samphire, sea plantain, sea beet and red valerian. A mallard once built her nest in a clump of valerian half way down the wall. You could have leant over and stroked her back. After dark, and when the tide is very high, hundreds of sea bristletails emerge from the cracks in the wall and scuttle over the stones.

Several times on a summer's morning, before 6 a.m., I have stood quietly by this wall and watched a kingfisher. It sits on the concrete pipe which brings the stream out below the conveniences. It dives repeatedly and returns to its unromantic perch. Mick Loates has seen it using an abandoned supermarket trolley as a perch. A few hours later hundreds of people are walking by. The kingfisher will be gone.

Back down by **Embankment Road**, the wall below the roadside path provides a botanical experience at any season. From the new year, cresses and dandelions start to bloom. In summer there are

51

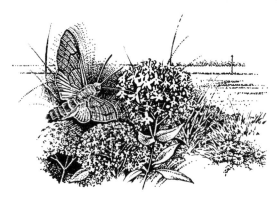

Hummingbird Hawk-moth (*Macroglossum stellatarum*) on Red Valerian

clumps of marjoram with its pink-purple flowers and aromatic leaves. Two naturalised plants are a feature; Mexican fleabane, a daisy-like flower growing out of the wall, and red valerian. The valerian is a big, bushy plant with showy, scented flowers that may be pink or white as well as shades of red. Sometimes, hovering in front of a valerian flower will be a humming-bird hawk moth; its grey body and chestnut-based, grey wings a blur of movement. In late summer, wild parsnip grows by the path. It is a yellow flowered umbellifer with leaves similar to those of its cultivated namesake.

You can walk down the pumping station slipway to the beach and along the foreshore to **High House Point** and **Bowcombe Creek**. By the pumping station lies the rudder and skeleton of an old ship, a reminder that the blocks of waterside flats have risen on the site of Date's shipyard. Dozens of schooners, for the fruit trade between Britain and the West Indies, were built here during the 19th century. From about 1830 to the 1880s **Salcombe** and **Kingsbridge** were the centres of a thriving ship-building industry.

The rocks above high water on the way to **High House Point** have typical maritime plants: thrift, sea campion, sea plantain and sea beet, rock spurrey and rock samphire. Close to the point, some kaffir fig, with thick, fleshy, three-sided leaves, cascades down a section of garden wall as if this were the Isles of Scilly.

From the shore an old stone landing place, **Southville Jetty**, juts out toward the main channel. Once it was a regular picking up call for the estuary paddle steamers. Now it is a strategic perch for fishermen and boats still use it for mid-tide landings.

While waiting on this jetty before a recent, memorable river trip with Tony Soper, a group of mature students was treated to a demonstration worthy of a television nature documentary. It was a warm December morning, with the sun shining. We, the students, were checking the waders out on the mud. Suddenly a group of dunlin and redshank took off, the redshanks yelping a warning. We looked around. There, flying over Tony Soper's approaching launch, was a peregrine.

With determined, deep wing beats, it flew on over the mudflats and swooped down towards a pair of shelduck. The shelduck stretched up their necks and the peregrine — it was obviously a young and inexperienced bird — swerved away. The predator gained height, climbed in a bow-bed and came into the attack once more. The sun glinted on the raised binoculars of our leader, as his launch drew closer. The next sortie was rapid and low. A curlew swayed its head out of line and must have felt the slip-stream. As the peregrine turned, it lined up on a heron, fishing at the water's edge, still as a post. Aware of the approach at the last moment, the heron ducked and squawked raucously.

The young *Falco peregrinus* now headed for a group of herring gulls sitting on the mud. The gulls took off. One of them made a neat 180 degree turn and started to follow the peregrine. With rather laboured wing beats the falcon climbed and veered to shake off the pursuit. The herring gull followed and was gaining. The hunter, pursued, climbed again but the gull continued to close the distance between them. The gull's beak opened and, unbelievably, it snapped it shut several times, only inches short of the peregrine's tail.

In our eyes, demoralised, it levelled out and made for the trees by the sewage works where it sat, hunched, near the top of a tree. The herring gull, having made its point, returned to the mudflats. As the launch crunched gently against the jetty, the question, in unison, was, 'Did you see that?!'

The seaweeds at **Southville Jetty** are unusually, for this estuary, dominated by bladder wrack, which has its bladders in pairs. Near here and on the weed-covered rock off **High House Point**, oystercatchers and turnstones often feed.

Either by the rough steps worn in the cliff at **High House Point**, or by the road, you can enter the quiet sanctuary of High House cemetery. Looking down the estuary from the edge of the cemetery a tongue of mud stretches south. Along the water's edge, either side of this tongue, waders, gulls and wigeon feed and rest. It is one of the most likely places to see bar-tailed godwits.

The cemetery is surrounded by evergreen holm oaks. Tree creepers, tits and goldcrests flit from branch to branch, greenfinches sing out their trilling and wheezing notes, pigeons and collared doves flutter in the canopy and a green woodpecker may swoop down onto the short turf. The gravestones and boundary walls are a lichenologist's heaven. A few minutes with a magnifying glass will reveal unexpected

Final resting place

beauties in these grey, green or orange crusty plants; unions of a fungus with an alga. In August and September, a forest of slender spikes, some six inches high, shoot up from the grass. Round them spiral small, creamy-white flowers. They are autumn ladies tresses orchids (*Spiranthes spiralis*). Each resembles a miniature, spiralling gladioli. In some years there are more than 1,000 spikes. They take about 22 years from germination to their first flowering. Soon after the orchids the grass erupts with fungi — spongy-gilled boletus, bright orange wax-caps and large, white milk-caps.

This cemetery is a beautiful and tranquil place, full of life and sheltered from all winds.

VIII

BOWCOMBE CREEK

Bowcombe New Bridge

If you have time only to look at one creek, it should be **Bowcombe**. New Bridge has carried the A379 across **Bowcombe Creek** since 1845. Initially the section nearest Charleton swung open, pivoting on 12 cannon balls, to allow barges up to the head of the creek. Under the bridge, at low water, you can see the mounds of lugworm casts, the spidery-topped tubes of sand mason worms and patches of orange sponge on the muddy gravel. The stonework of the bridge is encrusted with barnacles. They are mostly the Australian barnacle *Elminius modestus*. This species was recorded in the estuary in 1949 only two years after it was first seen in Britain. Near the base of the piers are some of the tall, conical barnacles *Balanus perforatus*.

From the bridge you follow the lane along the creek. Immediately on the left is a cascade of travellers' joy by the old quarry. Chiffchaffs sing here when they first arrive in March and April.

The wall between the creek and the road has an interesting flora. Whitlow grass and the ubiquitous hairy bittercress, followed by the taller thale cress, grow from February to April. In early summer, thyme-leaved sandwort and fern grass become dominant with red valerian, patches of yellow St. John's wort and a few plants of ploughman's spikenard following. In autumn the ivy is in bloom and attracts the late insects. In winter the lichens and mosses on the wall are at their best. The grey or blackish lobes, sometimes with rusty coloured tips, are dog lichens. The grey-green cups, like wine glasses, are pixie cup lichens. Two of the mosses have long, white hairs from the tips of their leaves. The low, green cushions, with upright, straight stalked spore capsules, are *Tortula muralis*. The domed cushions, with curved stalks burying the capsules in the cushion, are *Grimmia pulvinata*.

On the opposite side of the lane there are patches of winter heliotrope. Its scented, mauve spikes of blossom are out from Christmas until February. The rounded leaves enlarge during the summer to smother out other plants. Butterbur, its native relative, also grows at **Bowcombe**, along a damp section of the roadside verge, shortly before you reach the thatched cottage. It flowers a month or two later and its more ragged, rhubarb-like leaves grow big enough for it to have been used for wrapping pats of butter in pre-refrigerator days.

This lane has a good selection of umbellifers. The yellow-green umbels of alexanders are first out in April. The white cow parsley follows by May and rough chervil and the tall hemlock in June. Hemlock is the tallest plant along the lane. From the stately, smooth and purple-spotted stem sprout delicate leaves, like ferns. It is capped by spreading, white umbels of flower. But, although it looks handsome, it is deadly poisonous.

Common and rare cuckoo pint both grow by the roadside as well as balm-leaved figwort. The bright blue flowers of green alkanet, rising on sturdy stems from pointed, oval leaves, give a splash of spring colour.

Holly blue butterflies flutter by holly bushes or clumps of ivy. They are pale blue with scattered black speckles on the underside of the wings. Early in the year they lay their eggs on holly. When the next generation emerges they lay on ivy. Where oaks arch over the lane, you may see purple hairstreak butterflies, flickering grey above the leafy branches.

In autumn, pink jays pick the acorns from the oaks. You can see them flying across the creek with a nut wedged in their beaks. The white rump, black tail and blue-barred feathers on the wing make this the prettiest crow in Britain. The harsh shriek carries, startlingly, over the water. Ravens flap by with a throaty 'kronk' and buzzards wheel overhead mewing like cats. On autumn mornings wreaths of mist lie over the still water and swallows skim low; it is easy to see how people before Montagu's time imagined they hibernated in the mud beneath creeks and lakes.

56

The creek has almost all the common estuary birds and some rarities and the beauty of **Bowcombe** is that everything is so close. It is usually sheltered, even on a windy day when the rest of the estuary is swept by stinging rain driven by a stormy south-westerly.

On the mudflats a few curlew, oystercatchers and redshank feed. Along the edge of the channel one or two greenshank join them. On the raised mud bank, opposite the first bend in the road, gulls and oystercatchers rest. Most of the gulls are black-headed but, through the winter, there are also some common gulls. They are slightly larger, with greenish-yellow legs and bill, a domed head with grey flecking and slightly darker grey wings with no white leading edge. A few herring gulls may join them. George Montagu records how the juvenile herring gulls, which are fawn and speckled, used to be regarded as a separate species known as wagel gulls.

A heron frequents the creek. On one occasion a little egret flew in and settled near the heron. The heron stalked towards it and raised its wings, threateningly. The egret flew off; its round-winged, buoyant flight resembling a barn owl's and its black legs, trailing behind, showing yellow feet. Through the binoculars, in the same field of vision as the grey heron, was the white egret and, a sudden streak of vivid blue, a kingfisher.

As the tide begins to rise and comes flooding in under the arches of **New Bridge** the mud is covered. The curlew and oystercatcher move into the steep grass fields above the creek. The gulls take off and settle again on the water.

Bowcombe Creek, with New Bridge and the trees of High House Point cemetery behind and to the right

A cormorant will often swim or fly into the creek to fish until the tide ebbs. Montagu records the arrival of a cormorant at his house — 'it was placed on a stool in the library, where it adjusted its disconcerted plumage. We were astonished in a few minutes to see the stranger walk boldly into the room, while I was in conversation with a friend, and coming towards us with the greatest confidence and familiarity, joined us at the fireside. If it gets out of its pen, it walks direct to the house and enters the first open door without deference to anyone. It is extremely docile and of a grateful disposition, without the smallest tincture of a savage or vindictive spirit.' It was one of the many birds he kept in captivity to investigate the changes in plumage. Extra cormorants come to our estuary for the winter and recently one proved to have been colour-ringed as a nestling in South Wales.

Red-breasted mergansers also fish here in winter. The males look wonderfully photogenic, their shaggy-crested, green heads contrasting with the white neck and chestnut breast band. A few goldeneye regularly come and are sometimes joined by tufted duck. The commonest duck are the mallard, usually loafing under the far bank, under the overhanging oak trees, in pairs or groups, strung out down the creek. There may be more than 50.

The most endearing duck are the shelduck. There are usually a pair or two at **Bowcombe**. Nowhere else do you get such perfect views of the fluffy young shelduck, bobbing in the wavelets and marshalled by their protective parents. By early July nearly all the adults have left for moulting grounds in Bridgwater Bay or, perhaps, off the north coast of Germany in the Waddensee. A few stay on as 'aunts', supervising the créches of young birds, until they, too, leave in August.

At the head of the creek is a site where the resident pair of swans may nest.

Shelduck family, Bowcombe

It is hoped to build a bird hide, with access for the disabled, along **Bowcombe Creek**. From the hide you would be able to see up and down the creek and, in half an hour, most of the birds of the creek would walk, fly or float past.

By the roadside and on the bare patches on the paths and fields near Rose Cottage wormwood grows. It is a greyish weed about a foot high and smelling strongly of absinthe. In the fields, used by the free-range pigs, it is so dominant that the farmer, over more than ten years, has tried to get rid of it. He has cut it down, dug it up, applied weedkiller − all to no avail.

By these fields a public footpath goes up to the left and over to **Kingsbridge** giving good views on the way. To the right another footpath leads across a delightful saltmarsh. It has lush turf, with saltmarsh grass and saltmarsh rush. Together with the typical saltmarsh plants grows marsh arrow-grass. In the spring early scurvy grass grows by the handsomely restored little bridge that crosses the stream from **Shindle Mill**.

If you cross the bridge and turn back up the creek, the footpath climbs the sloping field southwards until it meets the lane just north of Charleton church. As you gain height, you see the whole estuary laid out in front of you. Each creek is a finger of sky-reflecting water, gently insinuating itself into the rolling hills of the South Hams and then ebbing back to Salcombe and the sea . . . where

'that which drew from out the boundless deep,
Turns again home.'

Common Buzzard

APPENDIX

Local societies and useful addresses

DEVON BIRD-WATCHING AND PRESERVATION SOCIETY
Membership Secretary, Gordon Vaughan, 58 Leeze Park, Okehampton.

DEVON WILDLIFE TRUST   188 Sidwell Street, Exeter.

KINGSBRIDGE AND DISTRICT NATURAL HISTORY SOCIETY
Martin Catt, 1 Higher Park, East Prawle, Kingsbridge.

KINGSBRIDGE – SALCOMBE FERRY SERVICE
apply 23 Embankment Road, Kingsbridge

SOUTH HAMS ENVIRONMENT SERVICE Follaton House,
Totnes. Their regular *Jigsaw* leaflet gives local environmental news
and details of walks and talks.

SALCOMBE HARBOUR MASTER   Whitestrand, Salcombe.

SALCOMBE FERRY OPERATING CO.   Boathouse, Fore Street,
Salcombe.

TONY SOPER (Occasional wildlife cruises)   Gerston Point, Kingsbridge.

ISLAND CRUISING CLUB   Island Street, Salcombe.

SALCOMBE YACHT CLUB   Cliff House, Salcombe.

SLAPTON LEY FIELD CENTRE (Field Studies Council)
Slapton, Kingsbridge.

COOKWORTHY MUSEUM, The Old Grammar School, Fore Street,
Kingsbridge.

COURTLANDS OUTDOOR ACTIVITIES AND FIELD CENTRE
Loddiswell, Kingsbridge.

OVERBECKS MUSEUM, Sharpitor, Salcombe.

SALCOMBE MUSEUM (Summer only), c/p David Murch,
St Davids, Herbert Road, Salcombe.

Further reading

MONTAGU, George 1802 and 1813
Ornithological Dictionary and Supplement
1803 *Testacea Britannica*
HAWKINS, Abraham 1819 *Kingsbridge and Salcombe with the Intermediate Estuary*
FOX, Sarah Prideaux 1864 *The Kingsbridge Estuary with rambles in the neighbourhood*
ALLEN, E. J. & TODD, R. A. 1900 *The fauna of the Salcombe Estuary* in Journal of the Marine Biological Association
CLEEVELY, R. J. 1978 *Some background to the life and publications of Colonel George Montagu* in Journal of Social Bibliography
HISCOCK, Keith et al. 1984 *Surveys of harbours, rias and estuaries in Southern Britain: Salcombe Harbour and the Kingsbridge Estuary* Produced by the Field Studies Council for English Nature
BORN, Anne 1986 *History of Kingsbridge and Salcombe*. Published by Phillimore, Chichester.
DEVON BIRD-WATCHING AND PRESERVATION SOCIETY publishes an annual *Devon bird report*
DEVON WILDLIFE TRUST 1991 *Nature in Devon*, an issue specially on estuaries
SANDERS, P. (editor) *The Soar bird report*, an annual report on the birds of the area from Salcombe to Hope Cove (available from the editor at 11 Saunders Way, West Charleton or from The Harbour Bookshop, 2 Mill Street, Kingsbridge).

AVERAGE NUMBER OF BIRDS SEEN IN ORIGINAL COUNT AREA BRITISH TRUST FOR ORNITHOLOGY ESTUARY COUNTS 1973–91

COUNTERS: Salcombe, South Pool and part of Frogmore **Val Mercer**
West side of estuary **Hilary and Tony Soper**
Original count area from east side of estuary **Bryan Ashby**
and **Gordon Waterhouse**

Many others help occasionally or have helped in the past, including: David Amas, Alan Doidge, Peggy Eagle, Ron and Liz Locken, Chris Pierce and William and Susan Topper.

/ means sometimes present but an average of less than 1.

+ means numbers are increasing

− means numbers have decreased

	J	F	M	A	M	J	J	A	S	O	N	D
GREAT NORTHERN DIVER+	1	1	/								/	1
GREAT CRESTED GREBE	6	7	5	3	2	/	/	/	1	2	4	4
LITTLE GREBE —	11	8	7						1	5	10	9
CORMORANT	8	10	12	9	8	7	9	12	19	24	21	15
HERON	5	5	5	6	4	6	8	8	7	8	5	4
MALLARD ad/juv +	42	23	23	13	15/7	14/6	18	34	57	59	55	43
TEAL	21	20	5	/				/	3	1	2	28
WIGEON	966	373	70	/					4	98	432	696
TUFTED DUCK	14	11	1	/							1	6
GOLDENEYE	28	21	7								3	19
RED-BREASTED MERGANSER	13	15	11	1	/					/	2	8
SHELDUCK ad/juv	189	205	140	108	52/3	26/16	8/13	10	3	6	49	136
BRENT GOOSE +	10	11	3								2	7
MUTE SWAN ad/juv —	23	21	19	21	17	19	20/5	19/5	23	24	22	21
OYSTERCATCHER	101	103	61	51	34	37	55	183	191	147	147	116
LAPWING —	84	34	1				4	32	22	9	27	24
RINGED PLOVER	1	1	/				1	16	4	2	1	1
GREY PLOVER	25	22	11	1	/	/	/	/	1	2	6	16
GOLDEN PLOVER —	167	114	140					3	21	97	150	211
TURNSTONE	18	17	17	5	/		/	3	1	8	12	15
CURLEW +	139	156	87	22	18	51	245	259	265	211	151	131
WHIMBREL				3	5	/	2	1	/	/		
BAR-TAILED GODWIT	7	5	2	2	1	/	/	/	4	5	6	4
COMMON SANDPIPER —	/	/	/	1	/		4	4	2	1	/	/
REDSHANK —	139	114	79	3	/	15	116	127	143	156	180	138
GREENSHANK	4	3	3	2	/	/	3	8	10	5	5	4
DUNLIN	541	440	95	4	5	/	16	25	39	38	182	491
GT BLACK-BACKED GULL +	183	35	17	8	2	6	5	5	5	21	15	70
LSSR BLACK-BACKED GULL	2	9	18	2	1	1	1	1	/	/	2	1
HERRING GULL	50	53	122	151	114	119	71	67	55	52	58	57
COMMON GULL	39	66	42	/			1	10	7	14	30	38
BLACK-HEADED GULL	786	802	529	51	15	40	758	1392	1452	1011	849	688
SANDWICH TERN				/	/	/	1	13	5	/		
KINGFISHER	/	/	/	/	/	/	/	/	/	/	/	/

The whole estuary was not covered until 1983. The Salcombe section brought in shag and kittiwake. Species to have significant increases from the original count totals were teal, grey plover and greenshank. The averages for 1983–91 are given below.

	J	F	M	A	M	J	J	A	S	O	N	D
TEAL	134	63	23	2					4	3	34	164
GREY PLOVER	56	38	27	/	/				/	2	15	32
GREENSHANK	17	13	11	6	/	/	5	12	22	14	19	15

Index

References to illustrations are in italics

63